DISCUSSION PAPER 75

# Self-Determination and Secessionism in Somaliland and South Sudan

## Challenges to Postcolonial State-building

REDIE BEREKETEAB

NORDISKA AFRIKAINSTITUTET, UPPSALA 2012

*Indexing terms:*
Somaliland
South Sudan
Independence
Self-determination
Secession
Nation-building
Political development
International relations
Comparative analysis

Language checking: Peter Colenbrander

ISSN 1104-8417

ISBN 978-91-7106-725-8

© The author and Nordiska Afrikainstitutet 2012

Production: Byrå4

Print on demand, Lightning Source UK Ltd.

# Contents

## Abstract

This paper analyses the notion of self-determination and secession by adopting a comparative perspective on two case studies, namely Somaliland and South Sudan. Somaliland declared its independence in 1991 following the collapse of the Somali state. Since then, Somaliland has been making relentless efforts to secure recognition from the international community. South Sudan successfully negotiated the right to exercise self-determination, a right that was formalised in the Comprehensive Peace Agreement (CPA) signed between the ruling National Congress Party (NCP) and the Sudan People's Liberation Movement (SPLM). The people of South Sudan held a referendum and voted overwhelmingly for secession, with formal independence being achieved on 9 July 2011. International law may better qualify Somaliland for statehood than South Sudan for three reasons: (i) it was created by colonialism, (ii) it has already been recognised, albeit only for a few days, as an independent state in 1960, and (iii) it has proven to be stable, functional and relatively democratic. Yet Somaliland has failed to achieve international recognition. This paper interrogates this discrepancy. It concludes that the existence of a partner ready to accept the right of self-determination, and geostrategic concerns about security as well as economic and political interests, determine international recognition.

Keywords: self-determination, secessionism, Somaliland, South Sudan, state-building

## Background

In 1897, Somaliland became a British protectorate (Spears 2010:121; Farley 2010:779; Bradbury 2008:26) and on 26 June 1960 British Somaliland got its independence[1] (Jhazbhay 2009; Hansen and Bradbury 2007: 463). Four days later, it joined Italian Somaliland upon the latter's independence on 1 July of the same year to form the Republic of Somalia (Farley 2010; Bradbury 2008; Hansen and Bradbury 2007). British Somalilanders pressed hard for the consummation of the union while the Italian Somalilanders wanted to proceed cautiously. Legislators from Italian Somaliland preferred to delay the union in order to settle pending issues. Apparently, British Somalilanders perceived postponement of the union could be to their disadvantage and pushed to accelerate it. 'I noted with alarm that the people of Somaliland had forced the union upon the South so precipitously that they alone had to pay the price by accepting a southern constitution, southern flag, southern capital and a southern Head of State – who also appointed a southern Prime Minister,' wrote Jama Mohamed Ghalib (cited in Spears 2010:129). In addition to the post of president, heavyweight ministerial posts were allotted to the Italian Somalilanders. British Somaliland held 33 seats in the 123-seat National Assembly (Spears 2010:129–30; SCPD 1999:14). This inequality eventually gave rise to a sense of loss and disaffection among Somalilanders (Bradbury 2008).

Presumably, it did not take long before Somalilanders discovered they had been mistaken in insisting on a prompt marriage without safeguards (Hansen and Bradbury 2007463; Pham 2010:140; Renders and Terlinden 2010:728–9). It became increasingly clear to them that the elite of Italian Somaliland would be in the dominant position (Hoehne 2006: 401). The post-independence constitution and political arrangements were set out according to democratic principles, however. Indeed, many perceive the period between 1960 and 1969 as a golden democratic age in Somalia's history (Samatar 2002; Hansen and Bradbury 2007; Bradbury 2008; Elmi 2010; Ismail 2010). Power-sharing between the two regions was arranged democratically, with the presidency reserved for former Italian Somaliland while the prime ministership was allocated to the erstwhile British Somaliland (Samatar 2008). This gave a semblance of equity between the parts. The reality, however, proved to be entirely different and generated a growing sense of marginalisation and alienation from the state among northeners. Moreover, the democratic system was rapidly faltering. Corruption and divisive clan politics soon ate into the system from within (SCPD 1999:15).

The double vices of pervasive corruption and divisive clan politics incited by

---

1.  It was recognised by 35 countries, including the United States and Israel, Benjamin R. Farley, 'Calling a State a State: Somaliland and International Recognition', *Emory International Law Review*, vol. 24, no. 2 (2010).

clan entrepreneurs running in the presidential election of 1967 (Farley 2010:781; Hansen and Bradbury 2007:466; Bradbury 2008:35) exposed Somalia to instability, jeopardised its integrity and state-building process and culminated in the assassination of President Abdirashid Ali Shermarke on 15 October 1969. Ultimately, clan politics coupled with sectarian political parties and widespread corruption created political chaos and gave rise to a military coup led by Gen. Mohamed Siad Barre in October 1969 (Spears 2010:118; Samatar 2008; Lewis 2002; Kusow 2004; Ismail 2010; Elmi 2010). The Supreme Revolutionary Council (SRC), established pursuant to the military coup, took over power from the political parties. The SRC targeted corruption, nepotism, anarchy and sectarian clan politics and was very well received by ordinary people on the streets for doing so (Spears 2010:133, SCPD 1999:15). Indeed, the Siad Barre regime declared clanism a cancer in society that had to be rooted out and embarked on a process of modern state-building (Bradbury 2008: 36). In its foreign policy, the Siad Barre regime established close relations with the Soviet Union. The Soviets, in turn, provided Siad Barre with training and armaments, which by 1972 were estimated to be worth $50 million (Khapoya and Agyeman-Duah 1985:23). The Barre regime is credited with bringing 'huge work projects, modernization efforts, and attempts to unify the Somali administration's two components' (Farley 2010:781–2). The regime's major success was believed to be in the education sector (Ismail 2010:110–12).

Nonetheless, the military rule of Siad Barre became increasingly repressive, as a result of which it alienated itself from the majority of the Somali people. Consequently, Siad Barre had to depend solely on his own clan (Farley 2010:782). Pervasive political repression by the regime and the accompanying economic and security deterioration provoked widespread dissatisfaction and rebellion, thereby undermining the project of state-building. The common understanding is that Siad Barre's downfall began with the invasion by Ethiopia in 1977 (SCPD 1999:16). Indeed, the defeat of Somalia in the Ethio-Somalia war of 1977–78 effectively brought about the demise of the Somali state (Walls and Kibble 2010:38; Mengisteab 2011:11). The first sign of fracture within the Siad Barre power system came when officers of his army led by Abdilahi Yusuf attempted to depose him following the Ethio-Somali debacle. The group of military officers behind the attempted coup were mainly from the Mejerteen clan, and their conspiracy against Siad Barre was crushed in 1978 (Ismail 2010:159). Thereafter, in revenge the regime perpetrated atrocities on the Mejerteen clan in Mudug and Bari regions (Elmi 2010:20). In reaction, the Mejerteen clan formed a rebel movement known as Somali Salvation Democratic Front (SSDF) to fight the Siad Barre regime (Møller 2009:18; Farley 2010:782).

Further repression and atrocities by Siad Barre's dictatorship led to the formation of other clan-based rebel movements in 1980 (Farley 2010). One of these was the Somali National Movement (SNM), founded in 1981 and supported by the Ethiopian government (Møller 2009:18; Mengisteab 2011:14; Renders and Terlinden 2010:727). The intra-state Somali war intensified throughout the 1980s. In a desperate measure to stay in power and to suppress the rebellion, the regime's army bombed towns indiscriminately. One such heavily bombed town was Hargeisa, the capital city of former British Somaliland, which was completely reduced to rubble (Walls and Kibble 2010:38; Hoehne 2009:258; Bradbury 2008:3). This act strengthened the determination of the SNM to not only depose the Siad Barre regime but also to reconsider the union of 1960. The immense suffering the Issaq clan were subjected to by the Siad Barre regime during the war and the domination of the Somali state by southerners finally convinced the Issaqs to opt for secession, with the idea of independence coming later.

The concerted struggles by various rebel groups eventually led to the collapse of the Somali state in 1991. While the United Somali Congress (USC) controlled the capital Mogadishu and southern Somalia (Renders and Terlinden 2010:728), the SNM controlled Somaliland and declared its independence on 18 May 1991, citing the fact that the territory was a creation of colonialism and as such was entitled to self-determination. The two factors that presumably triggered the declaration of independence at the Bur'o Conference were the unilateral formation of a government in Mogadishu by the USC without consulting the SNM, and popular pressure (Bryden 2004; Renders and Terlinden 2010). The USC's attempt to resuscitate the state following the collapse of the Barre regime reawakened the memory of southern domination among the Issaq clan.

The first two years following unilateral declaration of independence were fraught with conflict and war. This was, among other things, due to the minority non-Issaq groups who supported the Siad Barre regime and were still engaged in clashes with the Issaq dominated SNM (Renders and Terlinden 2010; Hoehne 2006:405). Following their takeover of Somaliland, however, the SNM chose to engage with these groups through negotiations aimed at reconciliation and the cessation of hostility and at avoiding destructive acts of retribution (Renders and Terlinden 2010:729). It could be said the Booroma conference constituted a watershed in the inception of the supra-clan, of the national recognition of Somaliland and of the formation of statehood (Renders and Terlindern 2010:731). The non-Issaq clans, albeit reluctantly, seemed to have accepted the idea of Somaliland statehood.

In 1993, the leader of the SNM asked clan elders to mediate between the feuding factions.[2] Consequently, the dominant Isaaq clan and the smaller Harti

---

2.   In an interview on 17 December 2011 in Hargeisa, the secretary general of the House of Elders and first secretary of the National Assembly of Somaliland explained to me how the guurti, clan elders, played a significant role in halting the war and achieving reconciliation among the warring factions.

(Dhulbahante and Warsengeli), Gadabuursi and Issa clans sent representatives to a conference of a national council of elders (*guurti*) in the town of Boorama, leading to the transition from military rule to civilian government (Walls and Kibble 2010:40). The *guurti* elected Mohamed Haji Ibrahim Egal (Renders and Terlinden 2010:731, Pham 2010:141) to the presidency in succession to the SNM leader. With the ascendancy of Egal as president, the SNM surrendered power to civilians. To propel the political process towards a non-clan pluralist system, President Egal announced the introduction of multiparty system in May 1999 (Kibble 2001:15). Aspiring parties were instructed to adopt an inclusive platform and avoid clan and religious affiliations and loyalties. In a referendum held in 2001, a new constitution was also adopted (Renders and Terlinden 2010:734), as was a bicameral parliamentary system, with the upper house for the *guurti* (elders) and the lower house an elected assembly (Pham 2010: 41; Renders and Terlinden 2010; Bryden 2004). Following the death of Egal, Dahir Riyale Kahin was elected president of Somaliland in 2003. This was followed by parliamentary elections in 2005 (Farley 2010:787). In a clear consolidation of the electoral and democratisation process, a presidential election was held in June 2010, as a result of which Ahmed Mohamed Mohamoud 'Silanyo' succeeded Dahir Kihale Kahin (Walls and Healy 2010). This peaceful and democratic transfer of power thereby enhanced the process of state-building.

Somaliland hoped that by embarking on the democratisation process, its chances of gaining international recognition would improve. Beyond sympathy from countries such as Ethiopia, Kenya, South Africa, Rwanda and the United Kingdom (Adam 2009), no country has to date formally recognised it (Walls and Kibble 2010:39; Farley 2010:784). For Somalilanders, the declaration of independence was not an act of secession, but was, rather, the reclaiming of a sovereignty they voluntarily gave up (Bryden 2004).[3] Relatively speaking, Somaliland is stable and power has been peacefully transferred in four democratic elections (Bradbury 2008; Pham 2010). This is attributed to the successful conflation of traditional clan structures and a modern representative polity, but also to 'avoiding revenge and achieving a successful reconciliation.' All this has 'allowed Somaliland to emerge as a political entity from a complex and highly destructive, conflict-ridden context, setting the *arena* in which statehood was negotiated' (Renders and Terlinden 2010:729). In this respect, clan structures have played a positive role. Clan mechanisms and institutions of conflict resolution have been decisive in, at least, mitigating conflicts and managing disputes and thus in bringing relative peace and stability. Undoubtedly, Somaliland has gone a long way towards state-building. Yet, the dispute with neighbouring Puntland over the Sool and Sanaag regions may undermine its quest for recog-

---

3.    Interview with members of parliament, 4–5 November 2010, Hargeisa.

nition (Bryden 2004; Renders and Terlinden 2010; Hoehne 2006), while recent positive changes in southern and central Somalia (Mosley 2012) may well complicate this quest. There is growing pressure on the government of Somaliland to join the process of reconstituting Somalia, as was seen at the London conference on this subject in February 2012 (Machar 2012).

Unlike Somaliland, South Sudan was not a colonial artefact. Nor was it properly integrated into the colonial state of Sudan. This seemingly contradictory historical trajectory makes the case of South Sudan theoretically challenging. Indeed, the British administered it as a separate entity within the colonial state of Sudan (Barltrop 2011:14). In fact, at some point they entertained the idea of joining it to their East Africa territories, Kenya and Uganda (Johnson 2003:10). The British colonial authorities governed Sudan through indirect rule, which in the case of southern Sudan meant that tribal leaders and customary law were used as political instruments of governance (Biel 2010:32). While indirect rule had the effect of internal disaggregation, it certainly fostered among southerners a sense of identity separate from that of the north. Many South Sudanese thus stress the referendum of 2011 as the fulfilment of the process of decolonisation that was denied to them in 1956 when Sudan became independent.[4] Like the Somalilanders, many South Sudanese invoked separate colonial rule to legitimise their quest for self-determination.

Separate colonial rule certainly influenced the place of southerners in the emergent postcolonial state of Sudan. Even on the eve of Sudan's independence, southern politicians expressed concern about their position in the soon-to-be independent Sudan. These concerns were twofold. The first was the relationship of independent Sudan with Egypt, as there was then talk of a union between the two countries, a cause championed by the Democratic Unionist Party (DUP) (Willis 2011:60). The second related to the possibility of their complete domination by the north. In order to avoid this, southern politicians convened a conference in October 1954 and demanded a federal system whereby the south would maintain self-rule (Daly 1993:11–3; Wakoson 1993:29; Johnson 2003:27). This demand was ignored by the northern political elite and eventually led to civil strife. Consequently, southern Sudanese were compelled to set about building their own state.

On 18 August 1955, a unit of southerners in the Sudanese army based in Torit, Equatoria mutinied. This event was prompted by the growing domination of the south by the northern army and the marginalisation of southerners (Johnson 2003:28; Barltrop 2011:15). The mutiny was quelled. Some of the mutineers fled into neighbouring countries, while others took refuge in the bush

---

4. Barnaba Marial Benjamin, minister of information in the government of South Sudan, interview, 12 August 2011, Juba, South Sudan.

to begin a guerrilla war. The guerrilla movement led by Joseph Lagu was to be known as Anyanya I. It lasted for 17 years and came to an end pursuant to the Addis Ababa agreement of 1972 between the southern movement and the military leader of Sudan, Gen. Ghaffar El Nimieri. This first attempt at self-determination ended with a negotiated self-rule arrangement. The prime provision of the agreement was the establishment of self-government of a united southern Sudan. The autonomous administration of southern Sudan retained the boundaries agreed upon at Sudan's independence. These border lines had been determined by the British, who had administered the two regions separately from 1899 to 1946 (Biel 2010:32). The autonomous administration was furnished with a High Executive Council (HEC) and a legislative branch in the form of a regional assembly (Wakoson 1993:32). The first president of the HEC was Abel Alier, who held the post between 1972 and 1978. In the election of 1978, Alier was replaced by Josef Lagu (Johnson 2003:42). Nonetheless, serious cracks emerged among the politicians of southern Sudan. A perception of domination of the autonomous region by the majority Nuer precipitated the conflict that contributed to the divisions in the region (Johnson 2011:126).

In 1983, ten years after the Addis accord, Nimieri abrogated the agreement. Southern Sudan was divided into three administrative regions against the wishes of the people, Sharia law was introduced and imposed on the people of the southern Sudan, the majority of whom were either Christian or followers of traditional beliefs (Wakoson 1993). This triggered a new intra-state war between south and north. The precipitant was a mutiny by an army unit in Bor, Upper Nile. Dr John Garang, a colonel in the Sudanese army, was sent to resolve the mutiny. Instead, Garang joined the rebels and founded the Sudan People's Liberation Movement-Army (SPLM-A) (Johnson 2003:61). This time the search for self-determination embraced the whole country with the aim of ushering in a new social contract whereby the state would be reconstituted as New Sudan. The notion of New Sudan (widely attributed to John Garang) was tied to the right of self-determination of all the people of Sudan, in contrast to the state. In terms of this vision, the liberation was envisaged of the entire population of Sudan from the grip of the Khartoum-based power elite that had suffocated the country since independence.

The signing of the Comprehensive Peace Agreement (CPA) on 9 January 2005, however, eroded this vision by affording the right of self-determination only to the people of southern Sudan. The National Democratic Alliance (NDA), a secular umbrella organisation that included the SPLM-A and could have realised the New Sudan Vision, was dismantled in terms of the CPA. The 22-year war ended with the signing of the CPA between the ruling National Congress Party (NCP) and SPLM-A (Grawert 2010; Deng 2010; Barltrop 2011). The chief provisions of the CPA were that southerners were to decide their future through a popular referendum to be held at the end of an interim period of six years; a simultaneous referendum would also take place in Abyei; consultative referendums were also scheduled for Blue Nile and South Kordofan; and wealth would be shared equally between Khartoum and Juba. In the interim, a government of national unity (GNU) would be established while the SPLM would form a government in South Sudan (CPA 2005). In compliance with the terms of the CPA, the referendum was held between 9 and 15 January 2011. The outcome was a resounding yes to secession, and consequently South Sudan became the 54th African state on 9 July 2011.

It is noteworthy that neither the SNM nor the SPLM openly advocated secession while fighting their respective adversaries. The SNM was caught between the choice of a failed union with the south or of a secession that was much less acceptable in Africa. Therefore, whatever desire for secession they had was kept secret, and their declared aim was deposing the Siad Barre regime and reconstituting the Somali state to achieve equitability in the representation of all clans and regions and in socioeconomic livelihoods. The SPLM also overtly struggled for a united and reformed Sudan. Its leader, John Garang, held out the vision of a New Sudan, for the achievement of which the SPLM worked with northern organisations under the umbrella NDA. Nonetheless, both movements ended by proclaiming secession and evoking the right of self-determination as the consummation of the process of decolonisation, but with one significant difference. The independent state of South Sudan was immediately accepted as a member of the international system of states. Somaliland, on the other hand, has been struggling for the last 20 years to achieve recognition. This discrepancy is what this paper will go on to explore.

The paper analyses the notion of self-determination and secession from the comparative perspective of Somaliland and South Sudan. The central question is what are the factors that facilitated recognition of South Sudan while hindering Somaliland in its pursuit of this objective? It also interrogates existing theories and international law to seek explanations for this anomalous situation. Specifically, it highlights the limitations of the theories, international law and international conventions in relation to self-determination and secession. The paper concludes that the existence of a partner (or the absence, in the case of Somaliland) in negotiations coupled with geostrategic, security, energy, economic and political interests determine the outcomes. The data for this article comprise interviews made during visits to the two countries, as well as published and unpublished material dealing with both cases. The visits to Somaliland took place between 4 and 9 November 2010 and on 16–17 December 2011. The visit to South Sudan took place between 3 and 21 August 2011. Beyond the literature on the specific cases, I have also examined the general literature on secession and self-determination in order to frame the two cases within a broader theoretical, conceptual, legal and historical dimension.

## Self-Determination: Theoretical Framework

The debate about self-determination can be divided into three broad categories: state-centric, society-centric and legalistic. This theoretical framework draws on these three categories. Self-determination and secession are two concepts that are intricately connected in the discourse on the formation of separate states. Separation supposedly takes place through severing relations with an already existing state. It may also take place with the dissolution of a state (Farley 2010:795). The conceptualisation of the right to self-determination varies greatly, depending on whether we are talking about the rights of the individual, group, ethnic entity or nation; or economic, cultural or political rights; or the right to autonomy, independence or union.

The moral, legal and political foundations underlying the discourse also diverge considerably, depending on political and ideological persuasions, extending from leftist (Marxist) to conservative to liberal. In Marxist literature, particularly as popularised by Vladimir Lenin (1974), Rosa Luxemburg and Joseph Stalin (1976), the right to self-determination, including secession, relates to oppressed nations and classes. Marxist notions of self-determination and secession, with their emphasis on class relations, contend that working class interests should determine the exercise and outcome of self-determination. Notwithstanding all these differences, however, the notion of self-determination seems to be grounded in a 'philosophical affirmation of the human drive to translate aspirations into reality, coupled with the postulates of inherent human equality' (Anaya 1996).

The criteria of statehood are invariably stated to be (i) territory, (ii) population, (iii) government, and (iv) independence (White 1981; Castellino 2008; Crawford 2006). Peoples who meet those criteria, in principle, should then be accorded international recognition. In its culturalist dimension, this strand of statehood inclines towards the perception that any culturally homogenous community deserves to form its own state in order to achieve congruence between the cultural and the political (Gellner 1983). This conception of self-determination prescribes that the seceding nation should meet certain conditions, notably cultural difference from the entity from which it is seceding. This conforms to the logic that multiethnic societies are inherently unstable and perhaps unable to sustain statehood. Thus, we have the perception that multiethnic states in Africa have failed or collapsed (Spears 2004, 2010).

Broadly, secessionism is defined as political withdrawal from an existing state (Tuttle 2004; Trzcinski 2004). In this definition, secessionism implies territorial disintegration, with the severance of part of the existing state's territory. The stipulation in this context is that the consent of the state that loses territory as well as international recognition is needed (Lemay-Hebert 2009:33). The political and legal implication of this stipulation is that unless the consent of the state that is losing land and citizens can be secured and concomitant international recognition is forthcoming, statehood is not feasible. This would reflect the situation of Somaliland.

There are a number of theories that grapple with the issue of self-determination and secession. These include democratic theory, liberal theory (Beran 1998), communitarian theory (Margalit and Raz 1990; Raz 1986), realist theory (Buchanan 1991; Shehadi 1993) and territorial justice theory (Lehning 1998). Democratic theory stresses the democratic right of people to govern themselves, the right of free political association; liberal theory advocates the right of the individual to determine her destiny; communitarian theory conversely seeks the right of self-determination in the collective, the nation. While realist theory focuses on the principle of the territorial integrity of states (Freeman 1999), territorial justice theory advances the idea that people have the right to supremacy in their territory (Steiner 1998; Castellino 2008). Other lesser known theories of self-determination are the theory of suffering and remedial theory (White 1981; Freeman 1999).

Arguably, underlying these theoretical persuasions is the notion of the moral and political rights to secession (Lehning 1998). Not every act of self-determination leads to secession. Indeed, self-determination could have the outcome of (a) emergence of an independent state; (b) free association with an independent state; (c) integration with an independent state (White 1981:149; Anaya 1996:84). The controversy pivoting around the concepts of self-determination and secession relates to whether it has universal value. The Wilsonian Doctrine confined self-determination to only European nations (Hobsbawm 1990:32, 102; Anaya 1996:76), while the post-Second World War debate on self-determination limited it to societies subjected to European rule, the decolonisation debate. The postcolonial debate declared self-determination to be a closed chapter (Anaya 1996:77). This declaration followed the end of European domination,

Colonial borders in Africa were accepted as sacrosanct and not to be tampered with. The principle of *uti possidetis* (Latin for 'as you possess') was enshrined in the Charter of the Organisation of African Unity (OAU) launched in 1964. In the African context, *uti possidetis* was interpreted to mean converting colonial borders into international boundaries (Farley 2010:802). The leaders who gathered at the historical launching of the OAU declared that 'all Member States pledge themselves to respect the borders existing on their achievement of national independence' (Temin 2010). All member states therefore committed themselves to the inviolability of colonially inherited territorial integrity (Makinda 1982; Spears 2004; Lemay-Hebert 2009; Ndulo 2010). The conflation of *uti possidetis* and the principle of territorial integrity ensured the preservation of the colonial territorial entity in Africa. *Uti possidetis* could also apply to secession, provided that secession leads to the restoring of a previous boundary (Farley 2010:804–5).

The most challenging debate in the discourse on self-determination relates to the contradiction between the principle of territorial integrity of states and fulfilment of the aspirations of aggrieved nations (Freeman 1999:365; Lehning 1998; Castellino 2008). Internationally, the principle of territorial integrity of states produced restrictive interpretations of the right to self-determination. This interpretation seems to stem from the values of peace and stability in the international order (Freeman 1999:357; Caney 1998:172–3). Furthermore, 'the limited likelihood any secessionist movement would be internationally recognized considerably reduces the appeal of local separatist strategies of power in normal times' (Englebert and Hummel 2003:31).

The political phenomenon known as secessionism has gained momentum worldwide following the collapse of the Soviet Union (Lehning 1998; Englebert and Hummel 2003; Weller and Metzger 2008; Kohen 2006). Political and economic factors play a significant role in territorial secession. Geographic location either facilitates or hinders secession, but also can have a significant impact on the functioning of the new state if secession takes place (Trzcinski 2004).

Whereas territorial secession would signify separation of part of a state from the rest of its territory, accompanied by political withdrawal by the separatist territory, cultural or ethnic secessionism can constitute a drive by a certain group for far-reaching autonomy within the state (Trzcinski 2004:208). The former will culminate in the emergence of a new nation state. In this sense, a distinction is made between territorial claims, which may lead to part of an existing state hiving off, and cultural claims, whereby a cultural or ethnic group seeks recognition and respect for its uniqueness, which may lead to self-rule.

The factors underlying demands for secession may vary considerably. Ethnic or cultural distinctions maybe invoked to drive the group's demands for self-determination. Past historical glories may be invoked. Further reference may also be made to subjugation. These drivers can be potent if the group occupies a distinct territory (Trzcinski 2004:208).

Invariably, conditions that determine the outcome of secessionist movements in Africa include:

- Interests of powerful states
- Attitude of the central government towards the secessionist movement
- Military balance between the secessionist movement and central government
- Strategic importance of the seceding region
- External support to the secessionist movement or central government
- Recognition of the secession by the international community, particularly the UN
- Economic significance of the seceding region for the parent state (Trzcinski 2004).

All these factors, as we will observe in the empirical cases, play a decisive role in the outcomes of people's aspirations. Theoretically, at least, in order to exercise the right to secession, certain conditions must be met. The UN International Covenant of 1966 declares, 'All people have the right of self-determination. By virtue of that right they freely determine their political status and freely pursue their economic, social and cultural development' (Freeman 1999:355). An earlier UN General Assembly Resolution 1541 (XV) concerning self-determination was adopted in reference to the decolonisation of peoples subjected to white domination (Castellino 2008:511). Yet the UN based its conviction on contradictory principles of reconciling the territorial integrity of states with the right of peoples to self-determination (Freeman 1999:358). The international regime governing the principle of self-determination is based on the traditional state-centred approach, according to which self-determination stems from the legitimacy of the state (Castellino 2008:501).

A recent trend, a humanitarian approach, however, appraises the right to self-determination as a fundamental human right of people (Anaya 2000; Hannum 1996). This is a profound shift from the familiar state-centred approach. Nevertheless, the humanitarian approach has already been subjected to scathing criticism on the grounds that it has nothing to offer the project of nation-state building, which is widely perceived as the most crucial problem in Africa (Zongwe 2010).

The theory of suffering postulates that if a people keep up guerrilla warfare for long enough, they will be rewarded with statehood (White 1981:154). The severity of a state's treatment of its minorities becomes a matter of international concern through remedial secession (White 1981:160; Lehning 1998; Anaya 1996). The theory of suffering is closely related to remedial theory. This upholds the right to self-determination in cases where serious and persistent violations of human rights exist, such as unjust conquest, exploitation and threat of extermination (Lehning 1998:2–3), and no remedy except self-determination is feasible (Freeman 1999:360). South Sudan is typically held to exemplify this theory. The voluntarist theory differs from the remedial theory, in that it holds that human rights violations are neither a necessary nor sufficient condition for the right to self-determination. It argues that nations have the fundamental right to self-determination (Freeman 1999: 360). This debate is also related to declaratory theory and constitutive theory (Crawford 2006). The former stipulates that statehood is an inherent right of any people, while the later attributes statehood to recognition by other states.

The notion of self-determination and secession faces a formidable challenge in the form of the notion of state sovereignty. States enjoy sovereignty: this is a function of equality of states, inviolability of their territorial integrity and political independence (Crawford 2006). Claims of secession thus assail the sanctity of the state as the basic unit of the international system (White 1981:162). Overall, sovereignty deals with the relations among states (Mamdani 2011). In this sense, it could be argued that statehood is externally oriented, particularly for purposes of legitimacy.

Cosmopolitan theorists such as Buchanan (1991), Barry (1991; cf., Freeman 1999) make secession conditional. The new state that is the result of secession must be able to provide peace, security and respect for human rights not only to the people within but also to those beyond its borders. In other words, the exercise of self-determination and secession is premised upon whether it leads to peace, security, stability, respect for human rights and development. The presumption is that if these conditions cannot be realised through secession, recognition may not be granted.

This is connected to another notion, namely people's wellbeing. This line of argument (Caney 1998) endorses national self-determination on the grounds that it promotes the wellbeing of people, an objective multinational entities supposedly cannot achieve. Both in an instrumentalist and intrinsic sense, the wellbeing argument justifies the presumption of secession (Caney 1998: 169). In terms of instrumentalism, self-determination and secession are presumed to bring autonomy and self-governance. And in terms of their intrinsic dimensions, they are presumed to effect self-fulfilment (Anaya 1996:107–9). In the principle of self-fulfilment as expounded by Hegel, the final destiny of a people is to achieve statehood (Crawford 2006).

In conclusion, self-determination that leads to secession is presumed to satisfy certain normative conditions. Firstly, it would bring peace, security, stability and development to the seceding people. The second condition is that it should, at least, not cause instability and insecurity to neighbouring people and beyond (Caney 1998; Lehning 1998). There are those who argue, however, that secession will not reduce violence (Spears 2010; Mayall 2008; Horowitz 2003). Rather, the argument runs, it has been shown in many cases that those seceding open new doors for minority claims to the right of self-determination and secession, thereby perpetuating conflict and violence.

## Comparing Somaliland and South Sudan

South Sudan was not a colonial creation in the usual sense, although it was ruled separately by the British until 1946 (Biel 2010:32), and neither is the territory inhabited by an ethnically homogenous society. It was poorly integrated into colonial Sudan, and the postcolonial state of Sudan did not do a good job to remedy this. Southern Sudan, therefore, remained marginalised and neglected throughout the postcolonial period.

Somaliland, on the other hand, was created as a territorial entity as a result of colonial action. Moreover, Somaliland is an ethnically, linguistically and religiously homogenous entity, though clan cleavages do exist: Somaliland comprises one major clan, Isaaq (70 per cent) and two other small ones, Harti and Dir (SCPD 1999:19). Economically, also, until recently all northern Somalis were pastoralists (Walls and Kibble 2010:2). Therefore, unlike South Sudan, Somaliland could reasonably claim the right of self-determination on several counts (Trzcinski 2004:210). Somalilanders meet one of the prescriptions in international law and international relations, namely the right of self-determination as peoples who were subject to alien rule. In addition, Somalilanders invoke another legal instrument, the fact that they were independent as a result of decolonisation for five days and gained UN recognition (Spears 2010:115). They voluntarily dissolved their independence to join in the creation of the Republic of Somalia (Bradbury 2008; Pham 2010; Ismail 2010). As they joined the union voluntarily, they retain the right to withdraw from it, their argument runs.[5]

In the case of South Sudan, the closest to a separate existence the SPLM could claim is the fact that the province was separately administered by the British, which, it is argued, entitles the territory to self-determination and secession (Englebert and Hummel 2003:34). The separate rule, however, was exercised within the Ango-Egyptian Condominium that replaced Turko-Egyptian rule and gave Sudan its modern shape (El Mahdi 1965). From an international law and international relations point of view, South Sudan represents a weak argument for self-determination and secession based on the decolonisation regime. Nonetheless, South Sudan received immediate international recognition while, 20 years on, no other country has recognised Somaliland. Why this discrepancy?

Somalis are the most homogenous nation on the continent of Africa with respect to ethnicity, religion, language, culture and mode of life (Walls and Kibble 2010; Bradbury 2008; Hoehne 2006). It was this homogeneity that in the first place induced them to seek a union of not only former Italian and British Somaliland, but of all Somalis as well, giving rise to Pan-Somalism (Lewis

---

5.    Interview by the author with parliamentarians of Somaliland in Hargeisa, November 2010.

2002). As Spears (2010) argues, it is only when the project to unify all Somalis failed that Somalilanders began seriously to entertain the idea of secession. This homogeneity may pose moral, philosophical and political challenges for those who contemplate recognition of statehood for Somaliland.

Arguably, there are certain conditions that render the case of South Sudan stronger than Somaliland's. One relates to the ethno-cultural dimension. The strength of South Sudan's claim to self-determination arguably emanates from ethno-cultural rationality. The ethno-cultural distance between its population and those who subjugate them was at least perceived by international actors as entitling South Sudan to statehood. Defining the disputants in terms of ethno-religious difference, notably the north as Arab-Moslems and the south as African Christians and animists, conferred a degree of legitimacy on the demands by the people of South Sudan to self-determination. This dichotomous presentation of identity in the Sudan has been criticised as simplistic and as misrepresenting reality (Harir 1994; Johnson 2003; Deng 2010). Yet this dichotomisation has been a powerful tool in certain conservative circles in the US, who forcefully argued for the secession of South Sudan. The logical solution was perceived by them to be self-determination and statehood, and an alternative narrative to suffering under an alien master might have opened the way for the principle of other remedial measures.

Referring to this fact, the president of the National Umma Party (NUP), Sadig Al Mahdi,[6] notes that the very elements of secession of South Sudan were implanted in the Comprehensive Peace Agreement. This was so because the partners in CPA, the ruling National Congress Party, the Sudan People's Liberation Movement and the international community, defined the conflict as religio-racial, that is as a people suffering under a religio-racial master. This perception not only made secession morally, legally and politically acceptable, but justifiable as well. The logic of this acceptance stems from the perception that a religio-racial group is subjected to extreme religious and racial domination and suffering, the relief for which can only be found in endowing the underdogs with the right of self-determination.

The second factor that worked in favour of South Sudan's claim to self-determination, in contrast to Somaliland, was the presence of a negotiating partner ready to engage in dialogue. In the case of South Sudan, there was a central government willing, albeit reluctantly, to accept the exercise of self-determination as well as the definition of the conflict in religio-racial terms. This paved the way for the eventual secession of South Sudan. In the case of Somaliland, there was no partner in the guise of a central government with which to negotiate. The consent of the central government is one of the key conditions for a successful

---

6.   Interview with the author, 24 May 2011, Omdurman, Sudan.

secession. No new nation has emerged in postcolonial Africa merely by military force without the consent of the metropolitan state. Accordingly, the international community has insisted that Somaliland seeks the consent of the rest of Somalia (Bryden 2004:29).

> Since declaring independence in May 1991, Somaliland has yet to be recognized by a single member of the international community, nor have any governments shown sympathy for its cause. To the contrary, most regional organizations and their members continue to uphold the unity of the Somali Republic. At the very least, they oppose Somaliland's 'unilateral' disassociation from Somalia, and insist upon a mutually agreed separation. After nearly a decade of waiting, however, many Somalilanders question for how much longer their sovereignty will remain the property of a state that no longer exists. (SCPD 1999:83)

It would have been extremely difficult for the AU, the UN and the international community to recognise the secession of the South Sudan but for the willingness of the ruling NCP in Khartoum to accept the outcome of the referendum. The absence of a central government in Mogadishu with which the victorious Somali National Movement (SNM) that declared independence in 1991 could have negotiated made it impossible for Somaliland to achieve recognition. The AU is captive to its Charter that celebrates the sacrosanctity of colonial borders and criminalises secession without the approval of the existing member state from which secession is taking place. For the UN also recognition of secession becomes problematic unless, of course, the demand originates with the AU. The case of South Sudan therefore had to pass through a number of legitimising stages: from Intergovernmental Authority on Development (IGAD) to AU to UN.

Furthermore, this divergence in outcomes relates to two crucial phenomena in self-determination, namely secession and dissolution. Secession relates to a state or condition where a territory and people secede from an existing state, whereas dissolution obtains as a result of the collapse and dissolution of a state (Farley 2010:795). Successful secession presupposes a negotiated settlement, often following devastating war. The SPLM was able to reach an accord with the ruling NCP in Khartoum whereby the people of South Sudan were permitted to determine their future through a binding referendum. The consensual Sudanese division of territory resulted in the redrawing of national boundaries under the CPA. Conversely, Somaliland declared its independence unilaterally after the Somali state collapsed, that is, as a result of state dissolution. Somaliland is therefore seeking an alternative to consensual separation because there is no existing state to recognise its independence. Yet there are those who argue that the emergence of Somaliland as a result of the dissolution of the Somali state conforms to international norms (Farley 2010:805).

Nevertheless, as was highlighted in the theoretical section, the interests of powerful states also play a decisive role in self-determination. In this sense, while South Sudan was fortunate to elicit the support of powerful states, particularly the US, Somaliland has not been able to do so. Probably two factors drove the US to actively engage in the self-determination struggle of South Sudan. The first is the abundance of oil in South Sudan and the second is geostrategic security interests. In terms of the latter, the conflict-ridden and sensitive nature of the region may have induced the US to craft a friendly state. This can be illustrated by the recent moves by AfriCom to establish bases in South Sudan and Uganda. Furthermore, conservative Christian fundamentalists in the US are also believed to have exerted significant influence on the White House. The Sudan Council of Churches (SCC), for instance, presented the struggle of South Sudan to the US public in terms of Christian-African against Moslem-Arab. This interpretation was adopted by conservative Christian organisations, which pressured the White House to support the SPLM (Mark[7] 2011; Brown 2011:44). With regard to statehood, what distinguishes South Sudan from Somaliland is that while the former meets all the criteria of statehood specified by White (1981), notably territory, population, governance and independence, the latter fails to meet the last criterion, independence. From a functionalist point of view, however, the state of Somaliland, after initial turmoil, has proven itself to be resilient and functional, while the state of South Sudan has been plunged into serious insurgencies and wars (although South Sudan is barely one year old), and thus has yet to prove that it is a functional state. A dimension that has, however, attracted widespread praise is that in its state-building process, Somaliland has successfully combined traditional institutions and authorities with a modern parliamentary system. This is widely credited with bringing relative peace and stability to the breakaway territory (APD 2006). Indeed, Somaliland's state-building process is sometimes seen as 'a first indigenous modern African form of government' (Kibble 2001:17).

The theory of suffering and remedial theory would also uphold the legitimacy of self-determination and secession in the case of South Sudan, but are of more tenuous utility in the case of Somaliland. These two theories taken together constitute a powerful theoretical tool in justifying South Sudan's secession. It is held that the people of South Sudan had been suffering too long at the hands of northern alien 'Arab-Moslems,' so that the conferring of independence on them was the only remedy for their suffering. In the case of Somaliland, it could not be argued convincingly that they had suffered under ethnically and religiously different people and that their independence was vindicated on those grounds.

Secession is complicated if certain people have to remain behind or, alter-

---

7.   Interview with author, 16 August 2011, Juba.

natively, find themselves involuntarily among those wishing to leave (Caney 1998:166). There is also a universal hesitation to divide a single people. It is this hesitation that Somaliland needs to overcome, because the division of an *ethnie* appears to be morally indefensible. According to this presumption, South Sudan's secession will be relatively smooth, since the division will be less painful. While the people and territory of South Sudan can be coterminous, that is no sections of South Sudan's people will be left behind in the north, cut off from their natural habitat, Somaliland would face a split among the Issaq, Harti and Dir clans. Even in South Sudan, it should be acknowledged that there are still disputes between Khartoum and Juba over boundary lines and border communities. One of the disputed areas awaiting resolution is Abyei, which the Dinka Ngok and Misseriya claim.

## Defining Separate Identity to gain Somaliland's Recognition

Especially where force is involved, nationalists are oft-times compelled to sell their narratives convincingly to the external world in order to elicit recognition of statehood (Tilly 1990). Unique identity is one of the presuppositions for a successful claim to the right of self-determination and secession. Identities are broadly perceived to be born out of social constructions (Smith 1986; Gellner 1983; Anderson 1991). The success in imagining and constructing a separate national identity may thus determine the final outcome of the endeavour to achieve statehood. This is so because a people's inherent right to statehood is no longer taken for granted, but has to be earned (Crawford 2006).

Furthermore, statehood may be determined by the degree to which we are able to convince others that we possess a separate identity. In this context, statehood is crucially founded on the construction of separate identity or, at least, on coherently formulating an identity that differentiates the emergent state from the old one from which it is separating. Success in convincing others of the existence of a separate identity reinforces the possibilities of secession. Convincing has two dimensions. One relates to self-convincing: the group has to be able to foster the strong conviction that it has a separate identity that unequivocally legitimises its search for secession and promotes perseverance in doing so. The second dimension is outward directed: it is aimed at convincing the external world (Crawford 2006).

Guided by these general principles, Somalilanders have over the last 20 years invested enormously in convincing themselves and the external world that they possess a separate identity that entitles them to be recognised as a sovereign state. The imagining and constructing of this differential identity has taken different forms. At least two claims have been expounded. One is the formal and legalistic claim, focused on Somaliland's legal entitlement to statehood. The other relates to the cultural dimension. Differences in culture and tradition are therefore presented as follows.

> During British colonial rule the Somalilanders, unlike Italian Somalia, were able to maintain their tradition, norms and values that makes them different from the South. This served them well to build institutions, local governance, peace, security and stability after they declared independence in 1991. It has also to be noted that Somaliland is not seeking separation. It was a state in 1960 that formed union with the South. Therefore Somaliland is claiming its rightful position in the international community.[8]

---

8.  Interview with Ahmed Dalal (Wiwa) Farah, director general, ministry of planning, government of Somaliland 5 November 2010, Hargeisa, Somaliland.

Therefore, there is no doubt that 'in Somalia, the northern secessionist territory that emerged in 1991 as the Somaliland Republic also traces its claim to sovereignty to the fact it was once a British colony whereas the south was administered by Italy' (Englebert and Hummel 2003:33). Since they embarked on the road to secession, Somalilanders have engaged in constructing narratives of a unique identity regardless of what detractors may think. In this narrative of constructing separate identities, the legacy of colonialism was invoked to serve a functional purpose (Hoehne 2006; Hansen and Bradbury 2007; Bradbury 2008). Drawing on the fact that international law, the UN and to certain degree OAU/AU charters uphold the right of peoples subjected to colonialism to exercise self-determination, Somalilanders maintain that Somaliland is a creation of British colonialism, akin to any state in Africa, and that therefore the decolonisation process has still to be fully consummated.

The fact that Somaliland disturbed the decolonisation process by voluntarily joining a political union in 1960 is simply explained as entitling its people to invoke sovereignty, so that they can voluntarily reignite the decolonisation process (SCPD 1999; Bryden 2004). To establish the statehood and independence of Somaliland on a legal and popular foundation, a referendum was held in 2001 to endorse a new constitution that asserted Somaliland's status as an independent state (Hoehne 2009:260; Bryden 2004:23). This was further buttressed by adopting and entrenching symbols of statehood: flag, national anthem, vehicle licence plates, national holidays, national currency, etc. (Bradbury 2008:4).

At the heart of Somalilanders' separate colonial legacy lies the presumed difference between Italian and British colonialism. The conservative British colonial practices of indirect rule were presumed to have given rise to a different identity from that in Italian Somaliland. In an interview on 5 November 2010 with Somaliland parliamentarians,[9] I was told that as a result of this colonial legacy Somaliland had evolved completely differently from Italian Somaliland. This difference, as mentioned earlier, was expressed in terms of governance, culture and language. As to governance, the legacy of British indirect rule is said to be in stark contrast to that of the Italians, chiefly in leaving intact local institutions, authorities and practices. In terms of culture and language also, it is presumed that Somalilanders have kept their language intact, so that today there is a clear difference between the language spoken in Somaliland and in southern Somalia: 'All the northern clans have the same dialect.'[10] The claims to language difference seem, at least to the outside observer, to be exaggerated. For Somalilanders, however, this is part of the cognitive construction of a na-

---

9.   In Hargeisa, Somaliland.
10.   Interview with Abdirahman Osman Aden, minister of foreign affairs of Somaliland until June 2010, Hargeisa, 2 November 2010.

tion. The nationalist narrative, of course, consciously and intentionally ignores certain facts. These include the fact that minority clans such as the Dhulbahane and Warsangeli do not share the narratives (Hoehne 2006:409–10; Hansen and Bradbury 2008:470; Renders and Terlinden 2010:740–1). As Renan (1991:11) in his seminal thesis, 'What is a Nation', already in 1882 noted, 'Forgetting, I would even go so far to say historical error, is a crucial factor in the creation of a nation.' Thus, states and nations are actually born out of a heavy dose of errors as well as selective constructions and readings of history. Somaliland is no exception to this rule.

The differential colonial legacy as told by Somalilanders has resulted in Somaliland's retention of traditional institutions, authorities and practices, which the country has been able to use successfully in its post-separation state-building endeavour. Furthermore, the retention of its precolonial dialect, which distinguishes Somaliland from the rest of Somalia, has enabled the former to construct a different cultural identity to buttress its statehood. All these factors are used to enhance the claim that Somaliland embodies a different identity from the rest of Somalia, and that this justifies secession. It is further argued:

> More significantly, the government maintained that its status as an independent state was not a violation of the OAU/AU's rules on the sanctity of African colonial/state borders; nor would recognition allow other regions to make similar claims to statehood. Because Somaliland had been a British Protectorate which, brevity notwithstanding, existed as an independent state prior to its union with the south, recognition would involve not a border change but the acknowledgement of Somaliland's previous colonial borders. And since independence would be the basis of colonial borders, no other community could make a similar claim to independence unless they could point to a prior colonial existence. (Spears 2010:161)

The reference to the colonial legacy also functions to justify the declaration of independence vis-à-vis international conventions. Since Somaliland is a creation of colonialism and since international convention allows people who have been subjected to colonial domination to be free, its secession would not constitute a breach of the OAU/AU Charter. Beyond the cognitive construction of separate national identity, Somaliland has also taken practical measures to reinforce its secession. It has set out to bring peace, security and stability; build national political institutions; and hold elections, all intended to strengthen the search for sovereignty.[11] It has incorporated clan structures, institutions, mechanisms and authorities into the governance system, and these have contributed to the relative stability and security prevailing in the country, although, as mentioned earlier, conflicts remain with the its eastern neighbour, Puntland.

---

11.   Interview with Ahmed Dalal (Wiwa) Farah, [incomplete??]

## Challenges of Recognition in Somaliland

A dominant doctrine, the root of which is to be found in the 18th century, and reminiscent of today's debate on self-determination, is that in order for a secessionist entity to be valid it needs to be accepted by the metropolitan state, otherwise it risks being declared illegal (Farley 2010:797). Katanga in Congo, Biafra in Nigeria, Anyanya I in South Sudan and Western Sahara were dismissed on account of this doctrine. Here, what is being distinguished is 'matter of fact' as against 'matter of law.' Through the latter, new states receive recognition from the international state system, a recognition that confers on them certain legal obligations and entitlements. As a matter of fact, states could achieve *de facto* existence, but could not join the international state system, which denies them legal entitlements and obligations (Crawford 2006). One of the underlying reasons Somaliland has so far not achieved recognition could be the influence of the doctrine of recognition by the metropolitan state.

In addition to the legal hurdles to recognition, there are other complicating factors. What facilitated technical and formalistic recognition of South Sudan's self-determination and ensuing secession is the existence of a legitimate central government that could be a credible and principled partner in the negotiations required to consummate the exercise of self-determination. In this sense, South Sudan met the condition that the contending parties should arrive at some kind of agreement if secession is to be finalised. The readiness, for whatever reason, of the ruling NCP in Khartoum to play a decisive role in negotiating the CPA between it and the SPLM has been noted above. The CPA therefore served as a legal instrument upon which the AU, UN and international community could depend to bestow recognition on the emerging sovereign nation state of South Sudan (Grawert 2010; Barltrop 2011; El-Affendi 2001). The same argument also extended to the recognition of Eritrea (Farley 2010:799).

Unfortunately, in the case of Somaliland, the central state collapsed, leaving a negotiating vacuum. As has been repeatedly intimated to the leaders of Somaliland, without the consent of the central government in Mogadishu it would be difficult to bestow recognition on the secession of Somaliland (Farley 2010). 'The international community tell us to first negotiat[e] with government of Somalia, they say if we agree with them it will be easy for the international community to recognise our independence'[12] (Bryden 2004:29). In short, the absence of central government, or the collapse of the state, on the one hand, facilitated the unilateral declaration of independence of Somaliland, thereby meeting the 'matter of fact' condition. On the other, this collapse meant that the

---

12. Interview with Abdirahman Osman, minister of foreign affairs of Somaliland until July 2010, Hargeisa, 2 November 2011.

'matter of law' condition could not be fulfilled and so became an impediment to achieving formal recognition. Mediation and roundtable dialogue aimed at resolving the problem was out of question because one partner was missing. IGAD, AU, UN and the international community, which played a decisive role in bringing the conflict in South Sudan to an end, could not contribute in a significant way in Somaliland, because they could find no legal basis for intervention. International law demands the consent of the central government from which secession is being sought if international bodies are to intervene (Trzcinski 2004). The case of Somaliland thus proved so sensitive that neither IGAD nor the AU would risk intervention. For neighbouring countries, Somaliland represents a complicated regional predicament, on account of the historical and ethnic configuration of their own societies.

Moreover, unlike South Sudan, what is conspicuously absent in Somaliland is the interest of powerful external actors. It is clear that geostrategic security, energy, political and economic interests determine the divergent international approaches. The discovery of oil in South Sudan profoundly changed the US's position towards the SPLM. Indeed the US did a U-turn in 1999. The CPA became feasible because powerful states were prepared to do what it took to enforce it. As Trzcinski (2004) has also noted, successful secession depends on the support of powerful external states with a vested interest in the emergent state. Somaliland has so far not been able to attract powerful state(s) to intervene on international platforms on its behalf, perhaps because it has no known strategic resources. The complicated relations of neighbouring countries with Somalia also affects Somaliland's chances of recognition. In addition to the implications of recognition of Somaliland for their own minorities, neighbouring countries are careful not to be seen to support the balkanisation of Somalia, while the international community is waiting for the AU to take the initiative. Thus, basically, recognition is predicated on a political rather than a legal rationale (Farley 2010:810).

# Conclusion

This paper has set out to analyse the notion of self-determination and secession by adopting a comparative perspective on Somaliland and South Sudan. It has argued that theories of self-determination and international law and conventions are of limited utility in tackling secessionism in Africa. It has further argued that geostrategic interests often determine the outcome of secessionist movement, as exemplified by the case of Somaliland and South Sudan.

Somaliland has been seeking international recognition for its sovereign statehood for the last 20 years without success. South Sudan, on the other hand, has already gained recognition. Comparatively, in terms of the international law on the self-determination of ex-colonial territories, Somaliland may have a stronger case than South Sudan, because Somaliland was the creation of colonialism while South Sudan was not. Moreover, Somaliland regained independence and achieved recognition in 1960 as a result of a decolonisation process that conferred statehood on it and placed it among the community of states. Somaliland unsettled the decolonisation and abrogated statehood voluntarily to found the Republic of Somalia. Another factor that may speak for recognition of Somaliland is that the country has proved itself to be more stable, secure and democratic than the rest of Somalia. It has also established a *de facto* or 'matter of fact' statehood. South Sudan has yet to prove that it can be stable and democratic. Although South Sudan is barely a year old, there are already signs that oblige it to prove it will become a respected member of the international community of states.

The discrepancy in outcomes can be explained from both a legal and international law perspective and in terms of geostrategic consideration. The factors that preclude recognition of Somaliland as a sovereign state include the absence of a central government in Somalia, lack of strategic resources and the homogeneity of Somalis. These same factors (presence of central state, heterogeneity of Sudan and strategic resources) facilitated the independence of South Sudan.

The theories of self-determination and secession are highly ambiguous, and it is high time that clear and coherent theories are found. International law and international relations are also extremely ambiguous when it comes to who has the right of self-determination and secession. The cases of Somaliland and South Sudan highlight the serious deficiencies in existing theoretical and legal instruments. This is further complicated by the dynamics of great power geostrategic, security, political, economic and energy interests. Those with strategic resources may be treated differently from those who lack them. As long as existing theoretical and legal instruments remain inadequate to addressing issues of self-determination and statehood, and outside geostrategic interests dictate outcomes, Africa will face serious challenges in its project of state-building.

# References

Adam, Hussein M. 2009. 'Somaliland and the Struggle for Nationhood: Review of Iqbal D. Jhazbhay's *Somaliland: An African Struggle for Nationhood and International Recognition*. http://www.pambazuka.org/en/category/books/60510/print, accessed on 27 September 2011.

Anaya, S. James. 1996. *Indigenous Peoples in International Law*. New York and Oxford: Oxford University Press.

Anaya, S. James. 2000. 'Self-determination as a collective Human Rights Under Contemporary International Law', in Pekka Aikio and Martin Scheinin (eds), *Operationalizing the Right of Indigenous Peoples to Self-determination*. Turko/Åbo: Institute of Human Rights, Åbo Akademi University.

Anderson, Benedict. 1991. *Imagined Communities: Reflections on the Origins and Spread of Nationalism*. London and New York: Verso.

APD (Academy for Peace and Development). 2006. *Dialogue for Peace, Local Solutions: Creating an Enabling Environment for Decentralisation in Somaliland*. Somaliland: APS Hargeisa.

Barltrop, Richard. 2011. *Dafur and the International Community: The Challenges of Conflict Resolution in Sudan*. London and New York: IBTauris.

Barry, Brian.1991. *Liberty and Justice: Essays in Political Theory 2*. Oxford: Oxford University Press.

Biel, Melha Rout. 2010. 'The Role of African and Arab elites in Building a New Sudan', in Elke Grawert (ed.). *After the Comprehensive Peace Agreements in Sudan*. London: James Currey.

Beran, Harry. 1998. 'A Democratic Theory of Political Self-determination for a New World Order', in Percy B. Lehning (ed.), *Theories of Secession*. London and New York: Routledge.

Bradbury, Mark. 2008. *Becoming Somaliland*. Oxford, Bloomington and Indianapolis, Johannesburg, Kampala, Nairobi: Progressio, James Currey, Indiana University Press, Jacana Media, Fountain Publishers, EAEP.

Brown, Timothy. 2011. Building Social Capital in South Sudan: How Local Churches Worked to Unite a Nation in the Lead up to the 2005 Comprehensive Peace Agreement. Unpublished paper.

Bryden, Matt. 2004. 'Somalia and Somaliland: Envisioning a Dialogue on the Question of Somali Unity', *African Security Review*, vol. 13, no. 2, pp. 23–33.

Buchanan, Allen. 1991. *Secession: The Morality of Political Divorce from Fort Sumter to Lithuania and Quebec*. Boulder CO: Westview Press.

Caney, Simon. 1998. 'National Self-determination and National Secession: Individualist and Communitarian Approaches', in Percy B. Lehning (ed.), *Theories of Secession*. London and New York: Routledge.

Castellino, Joshua. 2008. 'Territorial Integrity and the "Right" to Self-Determination: An examination of the conceptual tools', *Brooklyn Journal of International Law*, vol. 33, no. 2, pp. 499–564.

Crawford, James. 2006. *The Creation of States in International Law*. Oxford: Oxford University Press.

CPA. 2005. The Comprehensive Peace Agreement between the Government of the Republic of the Sudan and the Sudan People's Liberation Movement/Sudan People's Liberation Army. Nairobi, Kenya, 9 January.

Daly, M.W. and Ahmad Alawad Sikainga (eds). 1993. *Civil War in the Sudan*. London and New York: British Academic Press.

Deng, Francis (ed). 2010. *New Sudan in the Making? Essays on a Nation in Painful Search of Itself*. Trenton NJ and Asmara: Red Sea Press.

El-Affendi, Abdelwahab. 2001. 'The Impasse in the IGAD Peace Process for Sudan: The Limits of Regional Peacekmaking?', *African Affairs*, vol. 100, pp. 581–99.

El Mahdi, Mandour. 1965. *A Short History of the Sudan*. London, Ibadan, Nairobi and Accra: Oxford University Press.

Elmi, Afyar Abdi. 2010. *Understanding the Somalia Conflagration: Identity, Political Islam and Peacebuilding*. London and New York: Pluto Press and Pambazuka Press.

Engelbert, Pierre and Rebecca Hummel. 2003. Let's Stick Together: Understanding Africa's Secessionist Deficit. First Draft, prepared for African Studies Association 46th Annual Meeting, Boston, Massachusetts, 30 October–2 November 2003.

Farley, Benjamin R. 2010. 'Calling a State a State: Somaliland and International Recognition', *Emory International Law Review*, vol. 24, no. 2, pp. 777–820.

Freeman, Michael. 1999. 'The Right to Self-Determination in International Politics: Six theories in search of a policy', *Review of International Studies*, vol. 24, pp. 355–70.

Gellner, Ernest. 1983. *Nations and Nationalism*. Oxford and Cambridge MA: Blackwell.

Grawert, Elke (ed). 2010. *After the Comprehensive Peace Agreement in Sudan*. London: James Currey.

Hannum, Hurst. 1996 (revised edition). *Autonomy, Sovereignty, and Self-Determination: The Accommodation of Conflicting rights*. Philadelphia: University of Pennsylvania Press.

Hansen, Stig Jarle and Mark Bradbury. 2007. 'Somaliland: A New Democracy in the Horn of Africa?', *Review of African Political Economy*, no. 113, pp. 461–76.

Harir, Sharif. 1994. 'Recycling the Past in the Sudan: An Overview of Political Decay', in Sharif Harir and Terje Tvedt (eds), *Short-Cut to Decay: The Case of the Sudan*. Uppsala: Nordic Africa Institute.

Hobsbawm, Eric L. 1990. *Nations and Nationalism since 1780: Programme, Myth, Reality*. New York, Melbourne, Sydney: Cambridge University Press.

Ismail, Abdirashid A. 2010. *Somali State Failure: Players, Incentives and Institutions*. Helsinki: Hanken School of Economics.

Jhazbhay, Iqbal D. 2009. *Somaliland: An African Struggle for Nationhood and International Recognition*. Johannesburg: Institute for Global Dialogue and South African Institute of International Affairs.

Johnson, Douglas. 2011. 'Twentieth-century Civil Wars', in John Ryle *et al.* (eds), *The Sudan Handbook*. London: James Currey.

Johnson, Douglas. 2003. *The Root Causes of Sudan's Civil Wars*. Oxford: James Currey.

Khapoya, Vincent B. and Baffour Agyeman-Dua. 1985. 'The Cold War and Regional Politics in East Africa Africa', *Conflict Quartely,* vol. 5, no. 2, pp. 18.32

Kibble, Steve. 2001. 'Somaliland: Surviving without Recognition; Somalia: Recognised but Failing?', *International Relations*, vol. XV, no. 5, pp. 5–25.

Hoehne, Markus V. 2009. 'Mimesis and Mimicry in Dynamics of State and Identity Formation in Northern Somalia', *Africa*, vol. 79, no. 2, pp. 253–81.

Hoehne, Markus V. 2006. 'Political Identity, Emerging State Structures and Conflict in Northern Somalia', *Journal of Modern African Studies*, vol. 44, no. 3, pp. 397–414.

Kohen, Marcelo G. (ed.). 2006. *Secession: International Law Perspectives*. Cambridge and New York: Cambridge University Press.

Kusow, Abdi. 2004. 'Contested Narratives and the Crisis of the Nation-State in Somalia: A Prolegomenon', in Abdi Kusow (ed.), *Putting the Cart before the Horse: Contested Nationalism and the Crisis of the Nation-State in Somalia*. Trenton NJ: Red Sea Press.

Lehning, Percy B. (ed.). 1998. *Theories of Secession*. London and New York: Routledge.

Lemay-Hebert, Nicolas. 2009. 'Statebuilding without Nation-building? Legitimacy, State Failure and the Limits of the Institutionalist Approach', *Journal of Intervention and Statebuilding*, vol. 3, no. 1, pp. 21–45.

Lenin, Vladimir I. 1974. *Om Nationers Självbestämmanderätt*. Stockholm: Arbetarkultur.

Lewis, Ioan Myrddin. 2002. *A Modern History of the Somalia: Nation and State in the Horn of Africa*. Oxford, Hargeisa, Athens: James Currey, Btec Books and Ohio University Press.

Makinda, Samuel M. 1982. 'Conflict and the Superpowers in the Horn of Africa', *Third World Quarterly*, vol. 4, no.1, pp.93.103

Mamdani, Mahmood. 2011. 'South Sudan: Rethinking Citizenship, Sovereignty and Self-determination', Pambazuka News. http://pambazuka.org/en/category/features/72924, accessed on 17 May 2011.

Marchal, Roland. 2012. Somalia on Hold. Briefing Produced in May 2012. http://focusonthehorn.files.wordpress.com/2012/05/somalia-on-hold.pdf, accessed on 31 July 2012.

Margalit, Avishai and Joseph Raz. 1990. 'National Self-determination', *Journal of Philosophy,* vol. 87, no.9, pp. 439–61.

Mayall, James. 2008. 'Nationalism, Self-determination, and the Doctrine of Territorial Unity', in Marc Weller and Barbara Metzger (eds), *Settling Self-determination Disputes: Complex Power-sharing in Theory and Practice*. Leiden and Boston: Martonius Nijhoff.

Mengisteab, Kidane. 2011. 'Critical Factors in the Horn of Africa's Raging Conflicts'. *Discussion Paper no. 67*. Uppsala: Nordic Africa Institute.

Mosley, Jason. 2012. *End of the Roadmap: Somalia after the London and Istanbul Conferences*, Africa Programme Paper AFP PP2012/04. London: Chatham House.

Möller, Björn. 2009. The Horn of Africa and the US 'War on Terror' with a Special Focus on Somalia. DIIPER Research Series, Working Paper No. 19, Aalborg University.

Ndulo, Muna. 2010. 'Ethnic Diversity: A Challenge to African Democratic Governance', in Francis M. Deng (ed.), *Self-determination and National Unity: A Challenge for Africa*. Trenton NJ, Asmara: Africa World Press.

Pham, J. Peter. 2010. 'Somaliland: Book Review, *An African Struggle for Nationhood and International Recognition* by Iqbal D. Jhazbhay', *Journal of the Middle East and Africa*, vol. 1, pp. 139–44.

Raz, Joseph. 1986. *The Morality of Freedom*. Oxford: Oxford University Press.

Renan, Ernest. [1882] 1991. 'What is a Nation?', in Hombi K. Bhabha (ed.), *Nation and Narration*. London and New York: Routledge.

Render, Marleen and Ulf Terlinden. 2010. 'Negotiating Statehood in a Hybrid Political Order: The Case of Somaliland', *Development and Change*, vol. 41, no. 4, pp. 723–46.

Samatar, Abdi Ismail. 2008. 'Ethiopian Occupation and American Terror in Somalia', in Ulf Johansson Dahra (ed.), *Post-Conflict Peace-Building in the Horn of Africa*. Research Report in Social Anthropology. Lund: Lund University and Somali International Rehabilitation Centre.

Samatar, Abdi Ismail. 2002. 'Somalis as Africa's First Democrats: Premier Abdirazak H. Hussein and President Aden A. Osman', *Bildhaan* 2, pp. 1.64.

SCPD (Somaliland Centre for Peace and Development). 1999. *A Self-Portrait of Somaliland: Rebuilding from the Ruins*. Hargeysa, December.

Shehade, Kamal S. 1993. Ethnic Self-determination and the Break-up of States, Adelphi Papers 283. London: Brassey's for *The International Institute for Strategic Studies*.

Smith, Anthony D. 1986. *The Ethnic Origin of Nations*. Oxford and Cambridge MA: Blackwell.

Spears, Ian S. 2010. *Civil Wars in African States: The Search for Security*. Boulder CO and London: First Forum Press.

Spears, Ian S. 2004. 'Debating Secession and the Recognition of New States in Africa', *African Security Review*, vol. 13, no. 2, pp. 35–48.

Stalin, Joseph. 1976. *Marxism and the National-Colonial Question*. San Francisco: Proletarian Publishers.

Steiner, Hillel. 1998. 'Territorial Justice', in Percy B. Lehning (ed.), *Theories of Secession*. London and New York: Routledge.

Temin, Jon. 2010. 'Secession and Precedent in Sudan and Africa', *United Institute of Peace, Peace Brief*, no. 68, 17 November.

Tilly, Charles, 1990. *Coercion, Capital and European States, AD 990–1990*. Oxford: Blackwell.

Trezcinski, Krzysztof. 2004. 'The Significance of Geographic Location for the Success of Territorial Secession: African example', *Miscellanea Geographica* (Warsaw), vol. 11, pp. 207–217

Wakoson, Elias Nyamlell. 1993. 'The Politics of Southern Self-Government 1972–83', in M.W. Daly and Ahmed Alawad Sikainga (eds), *Civil War in the Sudan*. London and New York: British Academic Press.

Walls, Michael and Steve Kibble. 2010. 'Identity, Stability and State in Somaliland: Indigenous Forms and External Interventions', paper presented at Globalisation(s) of the Conflict in Somalia, University of St Andrews, 24–25 March 2010

Walls, Michael and Sally Healy. 2010. 'Briefing Note: Another Successful Election in Somaliland'.www.chathamhouse.org.uk.

Weller, Marc and Barbara Metzger. 2008. *Settling Self-determination Disputes: Complex Power-sharing in Theory and practice*. Leiden and Boston: Martinus Nijhoff.

White, Robin C.A. 1981. 'Self-Determination: Time for a Re-assessment?', *Alphen aan den Rijn XXVII-NILR*, pp. 147–70.

White, Robin C.A. 1981. 'Self-determination: Time for a Re-assessment?', *Alphen aan den Rijn XXVIII-NLR*, pp. 147–70.70.

Willis, Justin. 2011. 'The Ambitions of the State', in John Ryle *et al.* (eds), *The Sudan Handbook*. London: James Currey.

Zongwe, Dunia P. 2010. 'The Effectiveness of the International Community's Response to the Humanitarian Crisis in Darfur: A Legal Assessment', in Muna Ndulo and Margaret Grieco (eds), *Failed and Failing States: The Challenges to African Reconstruction*. Newcastle-upon-Tyne: Cambridge Scholars Publishing.

# DISCUSSION PAPERS PUBLISHED BY THE INSTITUTE

Recent issues in the series are available electronically for download free of charge
www.nai.uu.se

1. Kenneth Hermele and Bertil Odén, *Sanctions and Dilemmas. Some Implications of Economic Sanctions against South Africa.* 1988. 43 pp. ISBN 91-7106-286-6

2. Elling Njål Tjønneland, *Pax Pretoriana. The Fall of Apartheid and the Politics of Regional Destabilisation.* 1989. 31 pp. ISBN 91-7106-292-0

3. Hans Gustafsson, Bertil Odén and Andreas Tegen, *South African Minerals. An Analysis of Western Dependence.* 1990. 47 pp. ISBN 91-7106-307-2

4. Bertil Egerö, *South African Bantustans. From Dumping Grounds to Battlefronts.* 1991. 46 pp. ISBN 91-7106-315-3

5. Carlos Lopes, *Enough is Enough! For an Alternative Diagnosis of the African Crisis.* 1994. 38 pp. ISBN 91-7106-347-1

6. Annika Dahlberg, *Contesting Views and Changing Paradigms.* 1994. 59 pp. ISBN 91-7106-357-9

7. Bertil Odén, *Southern African Futures. Critical Factors for Regional Development in Southern Africa.* 1996. 35 pp. ISBN 91-7106-392-7

8. Colin Leys and Mahmood Mamdani, *Crisis and Reconstruction – African Perspectives.* 1997. 26 pp. ISBN 91-7106-417-6

9. Gudrun Dahl, *Responsibility and Partnership in Swedish Aid Discourse.* 2001. 30 pp. ISBN 91-7106-473-7

10. Henning Melber and Christopher Saunders, *Transition in Southern Africa – Comparative Aspects.* 2001. 28 pp. ISBN 91-7106-480-X

11. *Regionalism and Regional Integration in Africa.* 2001. 74 pp. ISBN 91-7106-484-2

12. Souleymane Bachir Diagne, et al., *Identity and Beyond: Rethinking Africanity.* 2001. 33 pp. ISBN 91-7106-487-7

13. Georges Nzongola-Ntalaja, et al., *Africa in the New Millennium.* Edited by Raymond Suttner. 2001. 53 pp. ISBN 91-7106-488-5

14. *Zimbabwe's Presidential Elections 2002.* Edited by Henning Melber. 2002. 88 pp. ISBN 91-7106-490-7

15. Birgit Brock-Utne, *Language, Education and Democracy in Africa.* 2002. 47 pp. ISBN 91-7106-491-5

16. Henning Melber et al., *The New Partnership for Africa's development (NEPAD).* 2002. 36 pp. ISBN 91-7106-492-3

17. Juma Okuku, *Ethnicity, State Power and the Democratisation Process in Uganda.* 2002. 42 pp. ISBN 91-7106-493-1

18. Yul Derek Davids, et al., *Measuring Democracy and Human Rights in Southern Africa.* Compiled by Henning Melber. 2002. 50 pp. ISBN 91-7106-497-4

19. Michael Neocosmos, Raymond Suttner and Ian Taylor, *Political Cultures in Democratic South Africa.* Compiled by Henning Melber. 2002. 52 pp. ISBN 91-7106-498-2

20. Martin Legassick, *Armed Struggle and Democracy. The Case of South Africa.* 2002. 53 pp. ISBN 91-7106-504-0

21. Reinhart Kössler, Henning Melber and Per Strand, *Development from Below. A Namibian Case Study.* 2003. 32 pp. ISBN 91-7106-507-5

22. Fred Hendricks, *Fault-Lines in South African Democracy. Continuing Crises of Inequality and Injustice.* 2003. 32 pp. ISBN 91-7106-508-3

23. Kenneth Good, *Bushmen and Diamonds. (Un) Civil Society in Botswana.* 2003. 39 pp. ISBN 91-7106-520-2

24. Robert Kappel, Andreas Mehler, Henning Melber and Anders Danielson, *Structural Stability in an African Context.* 2003. 55 pp. ISBN 91-7106-521-0

25. Patrick Bond, *South Africa and Global Apartheid. Continental and International Policies and Politics.* 2004. 45 pp. ISBN 91-7106-523-7

26. Bonnie Campbell (ed.), *Regulating Mining in Africa. For whose benefit?* 2004. 89 pp. ISBN 91-7106-527-X

27. Suzanne Dansereau and Mario Zamponi, *Zimbabwe – The Political Economy of Decline.* Compiled by Henning Melber. 2005. 43 pp. ISBN 91-7106-541-5

28. Lars Buur and Helene Maria Kyed, *State Recogni-tion of Traditional Authority in Mozambique. The nexus of Community Representation and State Assist-ance.* 2005. 30 pp. ISBN 91-7106-547-4

29. Hans Eriksson and Björn Hagströmer, *Chad – Towards Democratisation or Petro-Dictatorship?* 2005. 82 pp.ISBN 91-7106-549-

30. Mai Palmberg and Ranka Primorac (eds), *Skinning the Skunk – Facing Zimbabwean Futures.* 2005. 40 pp. ISBN 91-7106-552-0

31. Michael Brüntrup, Henning Melber and Ian Taylor, *Africa, Regional Cooperation and the World Market – Socio-Economic Strategies in Times of Global Trade Regimes.* Com-piled by Henning Melber. 2006. 70 pp. ISBN 91-7106-559-8

32. Fibian Kavulani Lukalo, *Extended Handshake or Wrestling Match? – Youth and Urban Culture Celebrating Politics in Kenya.* 2006.58 pp. ISBN 91-7106-567-9

33. Tekeste Negash, *Education in Ethiopia: From Crisis to the Brink of Collapse.* 2006. 55 pp. ISBN 91-7106-576-8

34. Fredrik Söderbaum and Ian Taylor (eds) *Micro-Regionalism in West Africa. Evidence from Two Case Studies.* 2006. 32 pp. ISBN 91-7106-584-9

35. Henning Melber (ed.), *On Africa – Scholars and African Studies.* 2006. 68 pp. ISBN 978-91-7106-585-8

36. Amadu Sesay, *Does One Size Fit All? The Sierra Leone Truth and Reconciliation Commission Revisited.* 2007. 56 pp. ISBN 978-91-7106-586-5

37. Karolina Hulterström, Amin Y. Kamete and Henning Melber, *Political Opposition in African Countries – The Case of Kenya, Namibia, Zambia and Zimbabwe.* 2007. 86 pp. ISBN 978-7106-587-2

38. Henning Melber (ed.), *Governance and State Delivery in Southern Africa. Examples from Botswana, Namibia and Zimbabwe.* 2007. 65 pp. ISBN 978-91-7106-587-2

39. Cyril Obi (ed.), *Perspectives on Côte d'Ivoire: Between Political Breakdown and Post-Conflict Peace.* 2007. 66 pp. ISBN 978-91-7106-606-6

40. Anna Chitando, *Imagining a Peaceful Society. A Vision of Children's Literature in a Post-Conflict Zimbabwe.* 2008. 26 pp. ISBN 978-91-7106-623-7

41. Olawale Ismail, *The Dynamics of Post-Conflict Reconstruction and Peace Building in West Africa. Between Change and Stability.* 2009.52 pp. ISBN 978-91-7106-637-4

42. Ron Sandrey and Hannah Edinger, *Examining the South Africa–China Agricultural Relationship.* 2009. 58 pp. ISBN 978-91-7106-643-5

43. Xuan Gao, *The Proliferation of Anti-Dumping and Poor Governance in Emerging Economies.* 2009. 41 pp. ISBN 978-91-7106-644-2

44. Lawal Mohammed Marafa, *Africa's Business and Development Relationship with China. Seeking Moral and Capital Values of the Last Economic Frontier.* 2009. xx pp. ISBN 978-91-7106-645-9

45. Mwangi wa Githinji, *Is That a Dragon or an Elephant on Your Ladder? The Potential Impact of China and India on Export Led Growth in African Countries.* 2009. 40 pp. ISBN 978-91-7106-646-6

46. Jo-Ansie van Wyk, *Cadres, Capitalists, Elites and Coalitions. The ANC, Business and Development in South Africa.* 2009. 61 pp. ISBN 978-91-7106-656-5

47. Elias Courson, *Movement for the Emancipation of the Niger Delta (MEND). Political Marginalization, Repression and Petro-Insurgency in the Niger Delta.*2009. 30 pp. ISBN 978-91-7106-657-2

48. Babatunde Ahonsi, *Gender Violence and HIV/ AIDS in Post-Conflict West Africa. Issues and Responses.* 2010. 38 pp. ISBN 978-91-7106-665-7

49. Usman Tar and Abba Gana Shettima, *Endangered Democracy? The Struggle over Secularism and its Implications for Politics and Democracy in Nigeria.* 2010. 21 pp. ISBN 978-91-7106-666-4

50. Garth Andrew Myers, *Seven Themes in African Urban Dynamics.*2010. 28 pp. ISBN 978-91-7106-677-0

51. Abdoumaliq Simone, *The Social Infrastructures of City Life in Contemporary Africa.* 2010. 33 pp. ISBN 978-91-7106-678-7

52. Li Anshan, *Chinese Medical Cooperation in Africa. With Special Emphasis on the Medical Teams and Anti-Malaria Campaign.* 2011. 24 pp. ISBN 978-91-7106-683-1

53. Folashade Hunsu, *Zangbeto: Navigating the Spaces Between Oral art, Communal Security And Conflict Mediation in Badagry, Nigeria.* 2011. 27 pp. ISBN 978-91-7106-688-6

54. Jeremiah O. Arowosegbe, *Reflections on the Challenge of Reconstructing Post-Conflict States in West Africa: Insights from Claude Ake's Political Writings.*
2011. 40 pp. ISBN 978-91-7106-689-3

55. Bertil Odén, *The Africa Policies of Nordic Countries and the Erosion of the Nordic Aid Model: A comparative study.*
2011. 66 pp. ISBN 978-91-7106-691-6

56. Angela Meyer, *Peace and Security Cooperation in Central Africa: Developments, Challenges and Prospects.*
2011. 47 pp ISBN 978-91-7106-693-0

57. Godwin R. Murunga, *Spontaneous or Premeditated? Post-Election Violence in Kenya.*
2011. 58 pp. ISBN 978-91-7106-694-7

58. David Sebudubudu & Patrick Molutsi, *The Elite as a Critical Factor in National Development: The Case of Botswana.*
2011. 48 pp. ISBN 978-91-7106-695-4

59. Sabelo J. Ndlovu-Gatsheni, *The Zimbabwean Nation-State Project. A Historical Diagnosis of Identity and Power-Based Conflicts in a Postcolonial State.*
2011. 97 pp. ISBN 978-91-7106-696-1

60. Jide Okeke, *Why Humanitarian Aid in Darfur is not a Practice of the 'Responsibility to Protect'.*
2011. 45 pp. ISBN 978-91-7106-697-8

62. Osita A. Agbu, *Ethnicity and Democratisation in Africa. Challenges for Politics and Development.*
2011, 30 pp. ISBN 978-91-7106-699-2

63. Cheryl Hendricks, *Gender and Security in Africa. An Overview.*
2011, 32 pp. ISBN 978-91-7106-700-5

64. Adebayo O. Olukoshi, *Democratic Governance and Accountability in Africa. In Search of a Workable Framework.*
2011, 25 pp. ISBN 978-91-7106-701-2

65. Christian Lund, *Land Rights and Citizenship in Africa.*
2011, 31 pp. ISBN 978-91-7106-705-0

66. Lars Rudebeck, *Electoral Democratisation in Post-Civil War Guinea-Bissau 1999–2008.*
2011, 31 pp. ISBN 978-91-7106-706-7

67. Kidane Mengisteab, *Critical Factors in the Horn of Africa's Raging Conflicts.*
2011, 39 pp. ISBN 978-91-7106-707-4

68. Solomon T. Ebobrah, *Reconceptualising Democratic Local Governance in the Niger Delta.*
2011, 32 pp. ISBN 978-91-7106-709-8

69. Linda Darkwa, *The Challenge of Sub-regional Security in West Africa. The Case of the 2006 Ecowas Convention on Small Arms and Light Weapons.*
2011, 39 pp. ISBN 978-91-7106-710-4

70. J.Shola Omotola, *Unconstitutional Changes of Government in Africa. What Implications for Democratic Consolidation?*
2011, 49 pp. ISBN 978-91-7106-711-4

71. Wale Adebanwi, *Globally Oriented Citizenship and International Voluntary Service. Interrogating Nigeria's Technical Aid Corps Scheme.*
2011, 81 pp. ISBN 978-91-7106-713-5

72. Göran Holmqvist, *Inequality and Identity. Causes of War?*
2012, 42 pp. ISBN 978-91-7106-714-2

73. Ike Okonta, *Biafran Ghosts. The MASSOB Ethnic Militia and Nigeria's Democratisation Process.*
2012, 64 pp. ISBN 978-91-7106-716-6

74. Li Anshan, Liu Haifang,Pan Huaqiong, Zeng Aiping and He Wenping, *FOCAC Twelve Years Later. Achievements, Challenges and the Way Forward.*
2012, 63 pp. ISBN 978-91-7106-718-0

75. Redie Bereketeab, *Self-Determination and Secessionism in Somaliland and South Sudan. Challenges to Postcolonial State-building.*
2012, 35 pp. ISBN 978-91-7106-725-8

www.ingramcontent.com/pod-product-compliance
Lightning Source LLC
Chambersburg PA
CBHW080210300326
41934CB00039B/3439